BOOK WORMS

GUESS WHO

Changes

Apple Jordan

mc Marshall Cavendish
Benchmark
New York

In the spring, my mom lays many eggs.

One of them is mine!

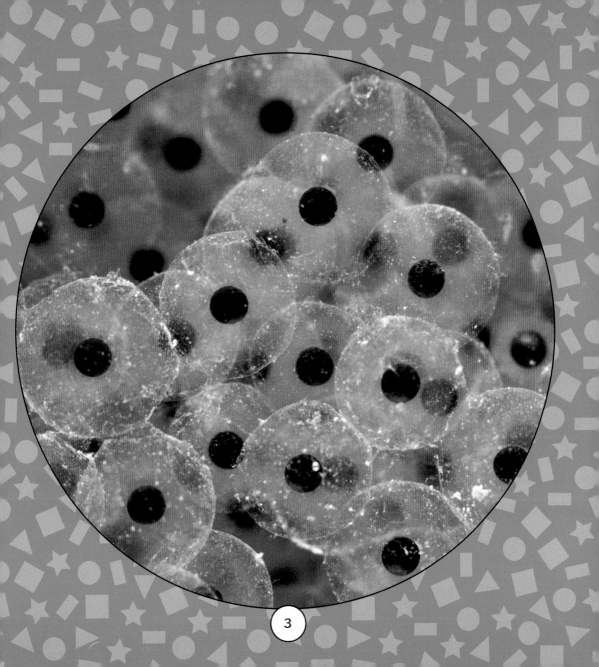

Jelly **covers** my egg.

It keeps me safe inside.

I grow bigger and bigger.

Before long I **hatch** from my egg.

The pond is my home.

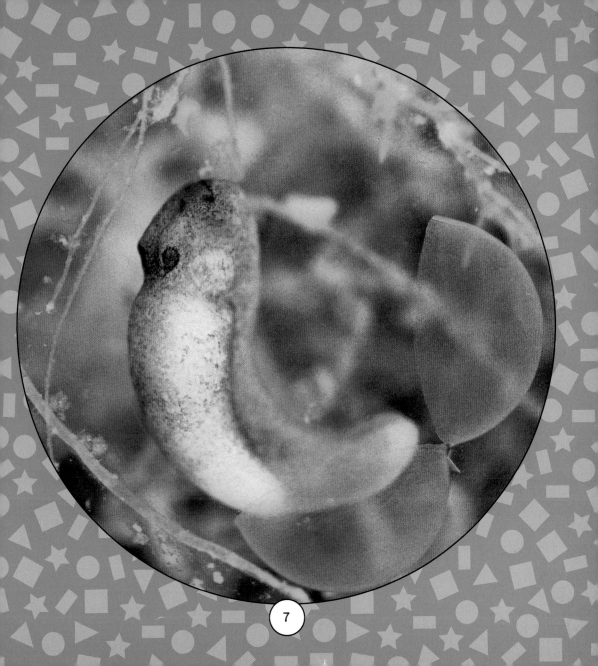

I have a long tail.

It helps me swim in the water.

Soon I start to change.

I grow two back legs.

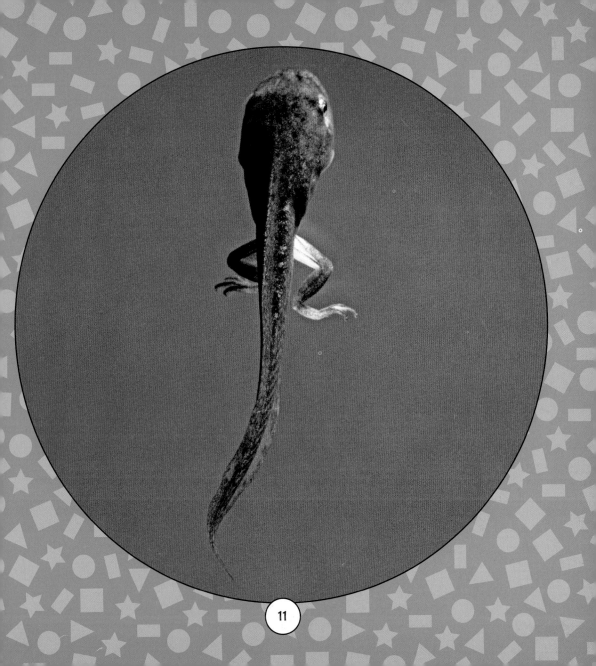

Then I grow two
front legs.

See how **different** I look!

My tail gets smaller.

Then it goes away.

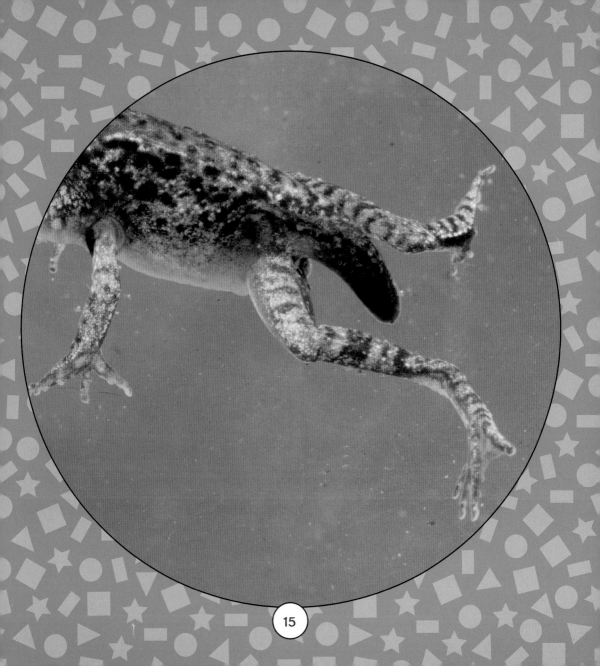

At last I can jump!

Who am I?

I am a frog!

Who Am I?

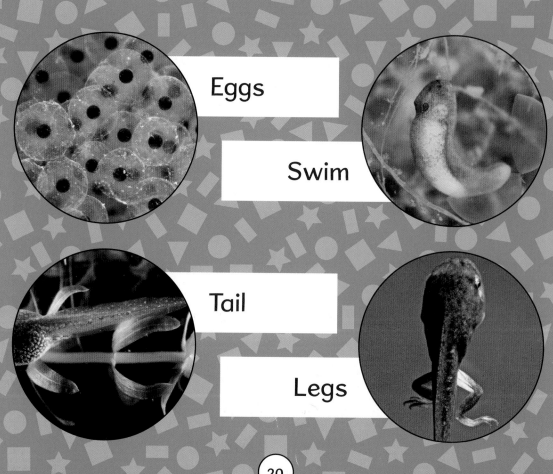

Eggs

Swim

Tail

Legs

Jump

Challenge Words

Cover (KUV-er) to coat

Different (DIF-er-uhnt) not the same

Hatch (hach) to come out of an egg

Index

Page numbers in **boldface** are illustrations.

About the Author

Apple Jordan has written many books for children, including a number of titles in the Bookworms series. She lives in upstate New York with her husband and two children.

With thanks to the Reading Consultants:

Nanci Vargas, Ed.D., is an Assistant Professor of Elementary Education at the University of Indianapolis.

Beth Walker Gambro is an Adjunct Professor at the University of St. Francis in Joliet, Illinois.

Other Marshall Cavendish Offices:
Marshall Cavendish International (Asia) Private Limited, 1 New Industrial Road, Singapore 536196 • Marshall Cavendish International (Thailand) Co Ltd. 253 Asoke, 12th Flr, Sukhumvit 21 Road, Klongtoey Nua, Wattana, Bangkok 10110, Thailand • Marshall Cavendish (Malaysia) Sdn Bhd, Times Subang, Lot 46, Subang Hi-Tech Industrial Park, Batu Tiga, 40000 Shah Alam, Selangor Darul Ehsan, Malaysia

Marshall Cavendish is a trademark of
Times Publishing Limited

Library of Congress
Cataloging-in-Publication Data

Jordan, Apple.
Guess who changes / Apple Jordan.
p. cm. — (Bookworms: guess who)
Includes index.
Summary: "Following a guessing game format, this book provides young readers with clues about a frog's physical characteristics, behaviors, and habitats, challenging readers to identify it"
—Provided by publisher.
ISBN 978-1-60870-425-5
1. Frogs—Juvenile literature. I. Title.
QL668.E2J67 2012
597.8'9—dc22   2011000330

Editor: Joy Bean
Publisher: Michelle Bisson
Art Director: Anahid Hamparian
Series Designer: Virginia Pope

Photo research by Tracey Engel

Cover: Papilio/Alamy
Title page: blickwinkel/Alamy

The photographs in this book are used by permission and through the courtesy of: *Alamy*: Barrie Watts, 3, 20 (top, left); Danita Delimont, 5; WildPictures, 7, 20 (bottom, left); Robert Clay, 11, 20 (bottom, right); blickwinkel, 13. *AnimalsAnimals*: O.S.F., 9, 20 (top, right). *Getty Images*: George Grall, 15; Stephen Dalton, 17, 21 (left); Michael Fogden, 19, 21 (right).

Printed in Malaysia (T)
1 3 5 6 4 2